Theory Time!

Step by Step Instructions for ABRSM and Other Exams

Grade 5

by

DAVID TURNBULL

CONTENTS

Bosworth

THEORY TIME!

Grade 5

The purpose of this series of books is to teach the principles of music theory. It is intended not only for pupils who want to pass theory examinations, but also for all those who would like to learn something about the theory of music as part of their general education. This book covers the new parts of the syllabus for Grade 5 of the Associated Board.

The sections of the book explain the ideas you need to know, and test your understanding with frequent questions. Write down the answers to these questions in the spaces provided, and then look up the printed answers.

You will notice that answers to questions are always printed on different pages from the questions themselves. The answers to Page 1 questions are in the margin of Page 2, for example, and the answers to Page 2 questions are in the margin of Page 1. Make sure that you look up the printed answers *only* after you have written down your own if you want to make good progress.

You can use this book with your teacher, who can set you pages to work through and then explain any difficulties you may have. Or you can use it to teach yourself, and you can use it for revision.

The sections of the book deal with different aspects of theory, but you need not work through to the end of each section before going on to the next. Your teacher may wish to recommend a different order of working — for example part of Section 1, then part of Section 2 before returning to complete Section 1.

Past examination papers are published by the Associated Board of the Royal Schools of Music and can be used for further practice, as can the series of books *Music Theory in Practice*, by Eric Taylor, also published by the Associated Board.

David Turnbull
Solihull, England, 1995

Acknowledgements

MISSA BREVIS: Gloria – Benjamin Britten
© Copyright 1959 by Boosey & Co.
Reprinted by permission of Boosey & Hawkes Music Publishers Ltd.

VESALII ICONES: St. Veronica wipes his face – Peter Maxwell Davies
© Copyright 1978 by Boosey & Hawkes Music Publishers Ltd.
Reprinted by permission of Boosey & Hawkes Music Publishers Ltd.

RITE OF SPRING: Sacrificial Dance – Igor Stravinsky
© 1921 by Hawkes & Son (London) Ltd.
Reprinted by permission of Boosey & Hawkes Music Publishers Ltd.

THE WASPS – Ralph Vaughan Williams
Copyright © Joan Ursula Penton Vaughan Williams. Publishing rights administered by Faber Music Ltd. for the UK, Republic of Ireland, Canada, Australia, New Zealand, South Africa, Israel and Jamaica. Printed by permission.
For all other countries, © J. Curwen & Son.

THEORY TIME! GRADE 5

Section 1 – Rhythm

Answers to questions on this page are in the margin of Page 2

Answers to Page 2 questions

Grade 5 time signatures

1 In addition to the times set for Grades 1–4, you need to know some of the irregular time signatures which composers sometimes use. The most usual of these are $\frac{5}{4}$, $\frac{5}{8}$, $\frac{7}{4}$ and $\frac{7}{8}$.

The upper figure tells you the *number* of beats there are in a bar. The lower figure tells you which *type* of note is used as the beat.

quintuple times

2 (a) How many beats are there in a bar of $\frac{5}{4}$ time? ____

(b) What type of note is used as the beat in this time? _____

(c) How many beats are there in a bar of $\frac{5}{8}$ time? ____

(d) What type of note is used as the beat in this time? _____

Times with five beats to a bar are called **quintuple times**.

septuple times

3 (a) How many beats are there in a bar of $\frac{7}{4}$ time? ____

(b) What type of note is used as the beat in this time? _____

(c) How many beats are there in a bar of $\frac{7}{8}$ time? ____

(d) What type of note is used as the beat in this time? _____

Times with seven beats to a bar are called **septuple times**.

Quintuple and septuple times behave as *simple* times, because their beats ordinarily subdivide into two or four. If beats are divided into three, triplet signs must be used.

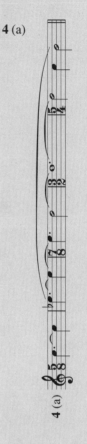

4 (a)

4 (b) Bar 1 $\frac{3}{16}$

Bar 2 $\frac{5}{16}$

Bar 3 $\frac{3}{16}$

Bar 4 $\frac{4}{16}$ (or $\frac{2}{8}$)

TEST 1 quintuple and septuple times

1 Write in time signatures for the examples below.
All start on the first beat of the bar.

Britten

(a)

Tchaikovsky

(b)

Britten

(c)

2 Insert any barlines necessary.
This starts on the first beat of the bar.

Ralph Vaughan Williams

*If you made any mistakes, read **1–2** again and do the test once more.*

International Copyright Secured

4 Time signatures may be altered during the course of a piece:

German trad.

(a) Complete the time signatures in this phrase:

Maxwell Davies

(b) Each bar of the phrase below needs a different time signature – write them in:

Stravinsky

irregular groups of notes

5 Triplets and duplets were explained in Grades 2 and 3. Other irregular groups in simple times which you may meet include:

(i) **quadruplet** – a group of four notes played in the time of three.

Chopin

(ii) **quintuplet** – a group of five notes played in the time of four.

Tchaikovsky

(iii) **sextuplet** – six notes played in the time of four – and

(iv) **septuplet** – seven notes played in the time of four.

Beethoven

(v) The figure 9 over a group of notes indicates that they must be played in the time usually taken by 8 notes of the same kind. It has no name.

Chopin

**TEST 2
irregular
note groups**

1 Insert time signatures and any missing barlines in the following, which starts on the first beat of the bar:

Chopin

2 Insert any missing rests at *:

Chopin

3 Insert any missing numbers over notes:

Moszkowski

If you made any mistakes, read the section again and do the test once more.

6 Practise writing four-bar rhythms, using the methods you have learned in Grades 1–4.

(i) Continue these phrases of which the openings are given:

(a)

(b)

(c)

(ii) Write four-bar rhythms, including in each the given rhythmic group:

(a)

(b)

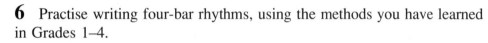

1 (a) C, D, B

(b)

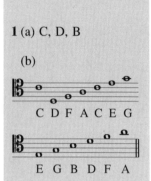

C D F A C E G

E G B D F A

TEST 3

1 (a) middle C
 (b) C
 (c) A
 (d) G
 (e) E♭
 (f) C♯
 (g) G
 (h) F
 (i) F♯
 (j) B

Answers to Page 3 questions

Answers to questions on this page are in the margin of Page 3

TEST 2

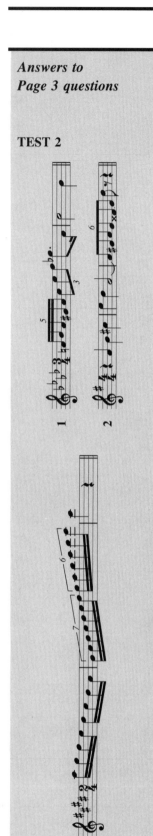

tenor clef

middle C

1 You need to know the notes in the **tenor clef**.

The clef is the same shape as the alto C clef, but the middle of the sign is written on the *second line down* of the staff. Notes on this line are **middle C**.

(a) What are these notes called?  *C, D, and B*

(b) Write under these notes their letter names, correct them if necessary, and learn them carefully.

Name C D F A C E G E G B D F A

Music for cello, bassoon and trombone is sometimes in the tenor clef.

tenor clef key signatures **2** Notice that in tenor clef key signatures, F sharps are placed on the second line up, and G sharps in the second space up, of the stave.

TEST 3 tenor clef notes

1 Name these notes:

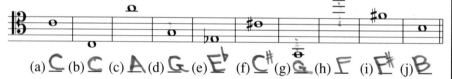

(a) C (b) C (c) A (d) G (e) E♭ (f) C♯ (g) G (h) F (i) F♯ (j) B

2 Rewrite in the tenor clef, but at the same pitch:

Mendelssohn

3 Rewrite in the alto clef, but at the same pitch:

Bach

If you made more than 3 mistakes, read over the page again and do the test once more.

Answers to questions on this page are in the margin of Page 6

Answers to Page 6 questions

8 (a) B   (b) C♯

(c) B♯ and C✕

new scales for grade 5

1 The new scales for grade 5 are the major and minor scales with key signatures of six sharps and six flats.

major scales – revision

2 Complete this table of key signatures with up to *five* sharps, putting in the keynotes of majors and relative minors:

Correct any mistakes you have made.

F♯

= g d a

3 (a) On which degree of B major will the scale which has six sharps in the key signature start? ___5th___

(b) What is the letter name of this new keynote? ___F♯___

(c) What is the sentence we have used to memorise the order in which sharps enter the series? ___Father Christmas gave daddy an easter bonnet.___

(d) What sharp is the sixth sharp in this series? ___E♯___

F♯ major

4 F sharp major has therefore six sharps:

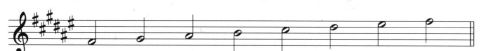

Name the interval between A♯ and B, and E♯ and top F♯ ___Major 1st___

5 Write F♯ major key signatures (a) in the alto clef, and (b) in the bass clef. After the key signatures, write the tonic of the major scale as a semibreve. Above each semibreve, write the sixth degree of the scale as a crotchet head.

(a)   (b)

f c g d a e

6 The sixth degree of a major scale is the keynote of the relative minor. What is F♯ major scale's relative minor? ___D♯ minor___

D♯ minor

7 D sharp natural minor ascends and descends using the sharps shown in its key signature.

8 (d)   8 (e)

9
(a)

(b)

10

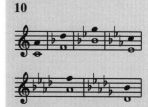

11 (a) the 4th
   (b) G♭
   (c) Battle Ends And
       Down Goes
       Charles' Father
   (d) C♭

12 (a)

(b)

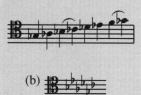

– D♯ melodic minor

8 Melodic minor scales descend in the same way as natural minors. When ascending they sharpen the 6th and 7th notes of the natural minor. Look at the scale of D♯ natural minor on the previous page.

What are the names of its (a) sixth degree? _B_ (b) seventh degree? _C♯_

(c) What will these sixth and seventh degrees be called when sharpened by a semitone? _B♯_ and _C𝄪_

Write out, using the clef, key signature and rhythms shown, the scales of D♯ melodic minor, (d) descending and (e) ascending:

(d)

(e)

– D♯ harmonic minor

9 Harmonic minors ascend and descend using the notes of the natural minor, *except for* the seventh degree, which is *always* sharpened..

Write out in crotchets, using the clefs shown, and using accidentals instead of a key signature, the scale of D♯ harmonic minor, (a) ascending and (b) descending. Slur the semitones:

(a)   (b)

scales with flats

10 Complete this table of key signatures with up to *five* flats, putting in keynotes of majors and relative minors:

Correct any mistakes you have made.

11 (a) On which degree of D♭ major will the scale which has six flats in the key signature start? _4th_

(b) What is the letter name of this new keynote? _G♭_

(c) What is the sentence we have used to memorise the order in which flats enter the series? _Battle Ends and down ____

(d) What flat is the sixth flat in the series, which must be present in the new key of G♭ major? _C♭_

scale of G♭ major

12 (a) Write out in crotchets, without using a key signature, the ascending scale of G♭ major. Slur the semitones. (b) Write the key signature.

(a)   (b)

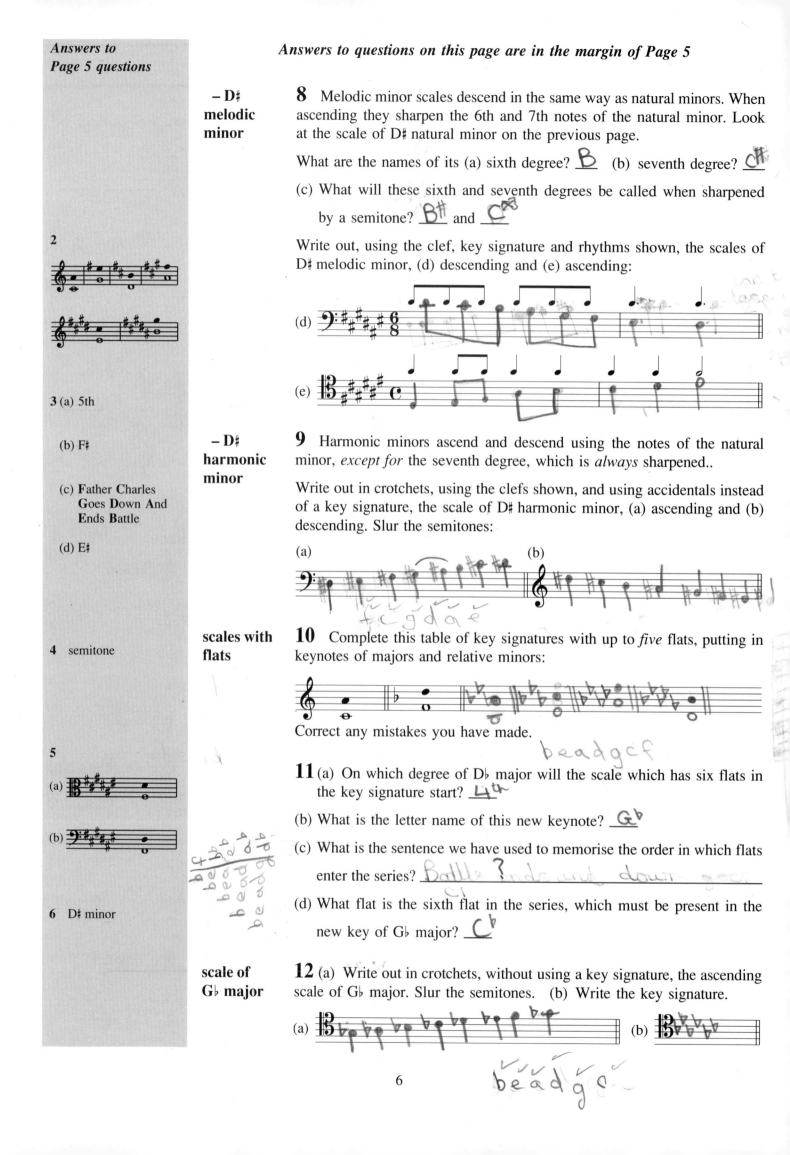

13 (a) Complete this table of key signatures up to and including six sharps and flats. Insert keynotes of major and minor scales:

(b) What is the keynote of the relative minor of G♭ major? ___E♭

E♭ minor

14 E♭ natural minor ascends and descends using the flats shown in its key signature, which is the same as G♭ major.

– natural minor

Write, with key signature and using the rhythm shown, the scale of E♭ natural minor ascending and descending:

– melodic minor

15 Read paragraph **8** again, then write out in minims, without the key signature, the scale of E♭ melodic minor descending and ascending:

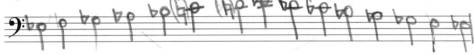

– harmonic minor

16 Read paragraph **9** again, then write out in crotchets, using the key signature, the scale of E♭ harmonic minor ascending and descending:

enharmonic equivalents

17 You have now learned about all major and minor scales which have key signatures of up to and including six sharps or six flats.

Notice that two of the major scales, F♯ and G♭ majors, *sound* the same although they are *written* differently:

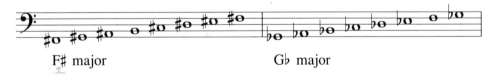

F♯ major   G♭ major

Scales (and notes) which sound the same but are written differently are called **enharmonic equivalents**. (See *Theory Time!* Grade 4, page 7).

D♯ minor and E♭ minor are also enharmonic equivalents.

Rewrite this phrase enharmonically in G♭ major:

18 Before you do the test on the next page, revise carefully page 21 in *Theory Time!* Grade 3, and pages 13 and 14 in *Theory Time!* Grade 4.

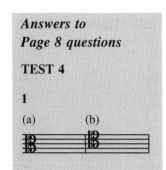
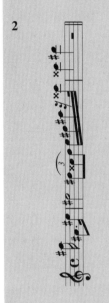

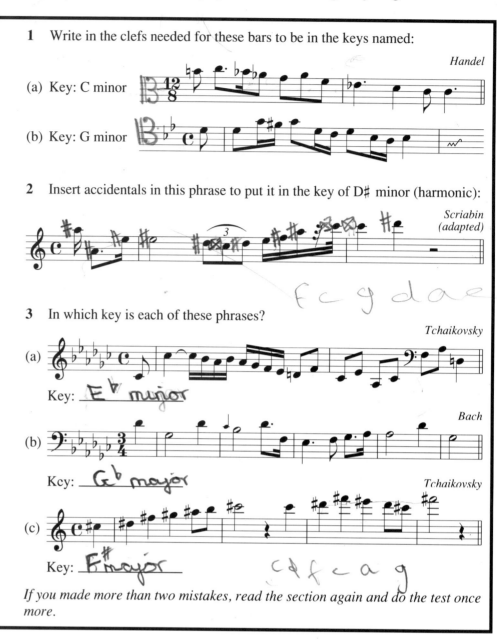

13 (a)

(b) E flat

14

15

16

17

TEST 4
keys

1 Write in the clefs needed for these bars to be in the keys named:

Handel

(a) Key: C minor

(b) Key: G minor

2 Insert accidentals in this phrase to put it in the key of D♯ minor (harmonic):

Scriabin (adapted)

f c g d a e

3 In which key is each of these phrases?

Tchaikovsky

(a)

Key: E♭ major

Bach

(b)

Key: G♭ major

Tchaikovsky

(c)

Key: F♯ major

c♯ f c a g

If you made more than two mistakes, read the section again and do the test once more.

Section ④ – Intervals

Answers to questions on this page are in the margin of Page 10

Answers to Page 10 questions

simple intervals

1 Revise carefully Section 4 in *Theory Time!* Grade 4.

All the intervals you learned in Grades 1–4 were intervals not greater than an octave. Intervals of an octave or less are called **simple** intervals.

compound intervals

2 Intervals greater than an octave are called **compound** intervals. Write below these intervals S (for simple) or C (for compound):

    (a) C   (b) S   (c) S   (d) S   (e) C

– number **3** To find the *number* of a compound interval, work in the same way as with a simple interval – count from bottom to top.

Look at (a) and (e) above. What are their numbers? 9 and 11

5 major 6th

– quality **4** Compound intervals, like simple intervals, can be perfect, major, minor, augmented and diminished.

Look at these simple and compound intervals in C major. The compound intervals in the lower row have the same *qualities* as the corresponding intervals in the upper row. You can call the first interval in the second row, for example, *either* a major 9th *or* a compound major second.

6 minor 9th *or* compound minor 2nd

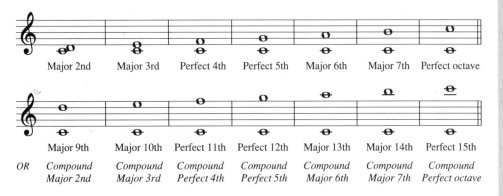

When deciding the *quality* of a compound interval, usually it is easier to think in terms of the corresponding simple interval.

Look at this interval:

(i) There are two names for the number of this interval – 10th or compound 3rd. Choose 'compound 3rd'.

(ii) Look at the lower note, D. Pretend that D is the keynote of the interval.

The third note in D major is F♯, but the upper note of this interval is F natural, a semitone lower than F♯.

Therefore the interval is minor – and can be called *either* a compound minor 3rd *or* a minor 10th.

TEST 5

1 (a) major 2nd
   (b) minor 2nd
   (c) major 10th
      (or compound
      major 3rd)
   (d) minor 10th
      (or compound
      minor 3rd)
   (e) perfect 11th
      (or compound
      perfect 4th)
   (f) minor 2nd
   (g) diminished 5th

2 (a) minor 3rd
   (b) augmented 11th
      (or compound
      augmented 4th)
   (c) minor 7th
   (d) diminished 4th
   (e) diminished 12th
      (or compound
      diminished 5th)

inversion of compound intervals

5 Compound intervals, like simple intervals, can be inverted, but one of the notes must be moved by *two* octaves:

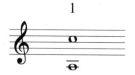

… when inverted become …

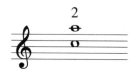

A compound interval and its inversion add up to 16. Compare this with a simple interval and its inversion, which add up to 9.

> **When inverted,**
> **major intervals become minor; minor intervals become major;**
> **augmented intervals become diminished;**
> **diminished become augmented;**
> **perfect intervals STAY perfect**

What is the number and quality of interval 2 above? *Major 6th*

transposition of compound intervals

6 Compound intervals may also be transposed to make them easier to name. *Both* notes must be altered in the same way, if necessary twice:

What is the number and quality of interval 1 above? *Compound M. 2nd*

TEST 5 intervals

1 Name the marked melodic intervals in this music by Bach:

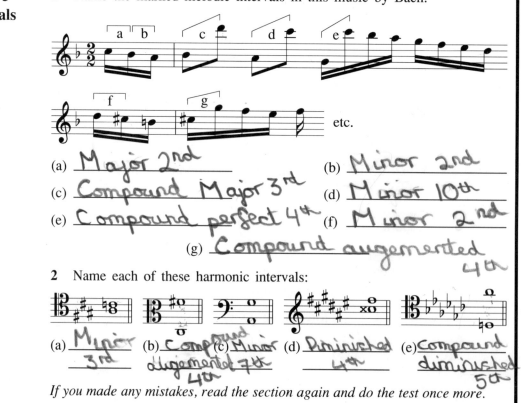

etc.

(a) *Major 2nd* (b) *Minor 2nd*

(c) *Compound Major 3rd* (d) *Minor 10th*

(e) *Compound perfect 4th* (f) *Minor 2nd*

(g) *Compound augemented 4th*

2 Name each of these harmonic intervals:

(a) *Minor 3rd* (b) *Compound augemented 7th* (c) *Minor 4th* (d) *Diminished 4th* (e) *Compound diminished 5th*

If you made any mistakes, read the section again and do the test once more.

2 (a) C

(b) S

(c) S

(d) S

(e) C

3 9, 11

Section 5 – Transposition

Answers to questions on this page are in the margin of Page 12

Answers to Page 12 questions

transposition 1 In Grade 3, you had to transpose melodies by an octave. Revise carefully
by an octave page 10 of *Theory Time! Grade 3* before continuing.

(a) Rewrite this phrase so that it is an octave lower, in the alto clef:

Schubert

3 (a) minor 2nd

(b) minor 3rd

(c) major 2nd

(b) Rewrite this phrase so that it is an octave higher, in the tenor clef:

Handel

etc.

2 In Grade 5, you will also need to transpose melodies by a major second,
by a minor third, and by a perfect fifth.

**Note that a melody in a major key can only be transposed to another
major key, and not to a minor key. Similarly, a melody in a minor key
can only be transposed to another minor key.**

4 (a) B♭ major

(b) B♭

(c) C

(d) C major

(e)

transposing Suppose you need to transpose this melody down a major second:
down a
major second

V I I V IV III IV II I

1 Decide the key of this melody. (a) What is it? **C major**

2 Write below each note the Roman numeral of its degree in the key –
the first two are done for you. (b) Write in the others.

3 Find the note which is a major second below the original keynote.

(c) What is it? **A B♭**

This will be the keynote of the transposed melody.

The first and second notes of the melody are V and I in C major.

(d) What are notes V and I of B♭ major? **F** and **B♭**

(e) Write them in on the stave below. Then write in the other notes in the
new key.

11

1

2 (a) C major

(b) I, V, IV,
III, IV, II, I

(c) B♭

(d) F and B♭

(e)

3 The method shown above is a safe way of transposing, but it takes a long time. You can use another method instead of always working by the numbers of the degrees.

Look at **2** again. Once the key and the degree of the starting note are established both in the original and the transposed versions, you can work by intervals.

Notes 2 and 3 are the same and are a perfect 4th above Note 1. Note 4 is a perfect 4th below Note 3. Note 5 is a major 2nd below Note 4.

What are the numbers and qualities of the intervals between:

(a) Notes 5 and 6? _Minor 2nd_

(b) Notes 7 and 8? _Minor 3rd_

(c) Notes 8 and 9? _Major 2nd_

The intervals between the notes of both original and transposed versions must be exactly the same.

Working by intervals is particularly helpful when the original melody contains many accidentals.

transposing up a major second

4 Paragraphs 2 and 3 have been about transposing *down* a melody by a major second. Now try to transpose a melody *up* a major second.

Purcell

(a) What is the key of this melody? _B♭ major_

(b) What note is its keynote? _B♭_

(c) What note is a major second higher than the answer to (b)? _C_

(d) Into what key must this melody be transposed so that it becomes a major second higher? _C major_

(e) Write out the Purcell tune above, in the new key.

transposing instruments 'in B flat'

5 Some instruments are called **transposing instruments** because the real sound of the notes they produce is different in pitch from the written notes.

The most common trumpets and clarinets in use today are called 'B♭' instruments, because the *written* note C will *sound* as B♭, a major second lower. All of the notes similarly sound a major second lower than written. The opening of the Purcell tune in **4** (e), when written in C major, is shown at (a); when played on a B♭ instrument, it will sound as shown at (b):

(a)   (b)

Answers to
Page 14 questions

concert pitch   The real pitch at which an instrument sounds is called concert pitch.

- Music for a B♭ instrument is written a major second higher than concert pitch.

- To find the concert pitch of music written for a B♭ instrument, transpose the written music down a major second lower.

In Grade 5 questions, you will always be reminded of the interval by which you transpose.

accidentals   **6**   If accidentals appear in the original melody, *equivalent* accidentals must appear in the transposed version. Remember that a *natural* is used to *sharpen* a flat, and to *flatten* a sharp.

(a) Transpose this phrase in D minor up a major second, into E minor:

(b) Transpose this phrase for B♭ clarinet down a major second. The start is given:

transposing by a minor third   **7**   Suppose you need to transpose this melody down a minor third:

Decide the key of this melody.   (a) What is it? _____

(b) Write under each note the number of its degree on the line provided.

(c) What note is a minor third below the original keynote, and therefore the keynote of the transposed version? _____

(d) Write on the stave the key signature of the new key, and then the notes of the transposed melody.

transposing instruments 'in A'   **8**   The melody in **7** is written for a clarinet 'in A'. In **5** you learned about clarinets in 'B♭', and that the concert pitch of their notes is a tone lower than the written notes. Clarinets in A are often used.

The concert pitch of notes played by instruments 'in A' is a minor third lower than the written notes. They are described as being 'in A' because the concert pitch A sounds when the player plays C.

8

9 (a) F major

   (b) V, I, III, V, V, IV, III, II

   (c) C major

   (d)

10 (a)

6

(a)   (b)

7 (a) E minor

(b) V, VI, V, III,
I, VII, I

(c) C♯

(d)

(a) This phrase is written at concert pitch. Transpose it a minor third higher, so that it is written correctly for a clarinet in A. Insert the new key signature:

Mozart

(b) Transpose this phrase for "A" clarinet a minor third lower, so that it is at concert pitch. The beginning is written for you. Be careful of accidentals.

Mendelssohn

transposing by a perfect fifth

9 To transpose music by a fifth, use the same method that you have used for transposing by a major second and a minor third. Decide the key of the music you are given, then the key a perfect fifth above or below it. Number the degrees of the notes in the original, and write in the notes in the new key. Check your answer by using intervals.

Suppose you are asked to transpose this phrase up a perfect fifth:

(a) What is its key? _____

(b) Write the degree of the scale under each note printed above.

(c) What is the key a perfect fifth higher? _____

(d) Write in the new key signature on the blank part of the stave above, followed by the notes of the melody in the new key.

transposing instruments 'in F'

10 The concert pitch of notes played by instruments 'in F' is a perfect fifth lower than the written notes. The commonest instruments 'in F' are the horn in F, and the cor anglais.

(a) Transpose this phrase written for a horn in F down a perfect fifth, so that it is written at concert pitch. Write in the new key signature.

Tchaikovsky

(b) Transpose this passage at concert pitch up a perfect fifth, so that it is written at the correct pitch for cor anglais. Write in the new key signature.

Dvořák

11   Some music is not written in a key. In any case where the key cannot be identified, **you will have to work entirely by intervals.**

Here is a row of notes by Berg:

In free time

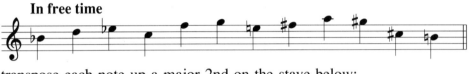

transpose each note up a major 2nd on the stave below:

TEST 6 transposition

1 Transpose this passage at concert pitch up a major second, for B♭ trumpet.

Tchaikovsky

2 What note, at concert pitch, will sound if:

   (a) A trumpet in A plays a written C? ___

   (b) A horn in F plays a written C? ___

   (c) A clarinet in B♭ plays a written C? ___

3 *Without using a key signature,* transpose this phrase for B♭ clarinet down a major second so that it is written at concert pitch:

Brahms

If you made a mistake, look at the appropriate paragraph again.

3

4

(a)

    I II IV V

(b)

    I II IV V

(c)

    I II IV V

6 (a) $\frac{6}{4}$

   (b) $\frac{5}{3}$

   (c) $\frac{6}{3}$

Answers to questions on this page are in the margin of Page 15

Answers to Page 15 questions

10 (b)

11

TEST 6 Answers

1

2 (a) A

(b) F

(c) B♭

3

---

triads in root position – $\frac{5}{3}$ chord

1 Look at the tonic triad of C major. Its lowest note, called the root, is C. The middle note is E, a *third* above C. The top note is G – a *fifth* above the root.

It is called a *five-three* ($\frac{5}{3}$) chord. It is also said to be in **root position**.

2 In Grade 4 you need to be able to write triads I, IV and V in keys up to five sharps and five flats. For Grade 5, you must know triads I, IV, V **and triad II** in keys up to and including **six** sharps and flats.

3 Triad II is the triad on the supertonic. Here it is in C major, written as a $\frac{5}{3}$ chord. After it, write II in A harmonic minor.

4 Write out triads I, II, IV and V as $\frac{5}{3}$ chords in each of the keys given below. Use the clefs shown and write under each chord its Roman number.

(a) F♯ major   (b) G♭ major   (c) D♯ harmonic minor

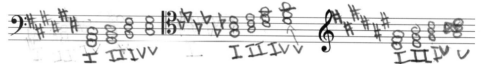

inversion of triads

5 A triad, like an interval, can be inverted. At (a) is the triad of C major written as a $\frac{5}{3}$ chord. At (b) it is inverted, with C moved from the bottom of the chord to the top.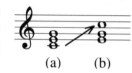

first inversion – $\frac{6}{3}$ chord

In this **first inversion** of the triad, the middle note is a *third* above the bottom note and the top note is a *sixth* above the bottom note. It is called *six-three* ($\frac{6}{3}$) chord.

second inversion – $\frac{6}{4}$ chord

6 You can also write a **second inversion** of the triad, in which the lowest note is G, the middle note is C, and the top note is E.

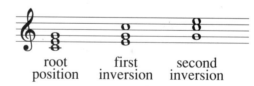

root position   first inversion   second inversion

In this second inversion, the middle note is a *fourth* above the bottom note and the top note is a *sixth* above the bottom note. It is called *six-four* ($\frac{6}{4}$) chord.

Here, in its three possible arrangements, is the tonic triad of D major. Write under each whether it is a $\frac{5}{3}$, $\frac{6}{3}$ or $\frac{6}{4}$ chord:

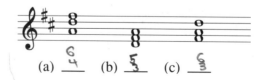

(a) ___   (b) ___   (c) ___

naming inversions

7 In Grade 5, you must know the root position and *both* inversions of tonic triads, and the root position and *first* inversions of II, IV and V.

Here are three other ways used to describe the inversions of triads.

A Letters can be used to show the position of the triad – 'a' for root position (the $\frac{5}{3}$ chord); 'b' for first inversion (the $\frac{6}{3}$ chord); 'c' for second inversion (the $\frac{6}{4}$ chord). For example, Ic means the tonic triad of a key in second inversion.

*Notice, though, that for root position chords the 'a' is often left out – the Roman number with no letter after it means that the triad is in **root position**.*

(a) What is the meaning of IVb? ~~Supdominatriad in its~~ *first inversion*

(b) What is the meaning of II? ~~Supertonic triad in~~ *root position*

B Another way is to describe the lowest note.
(a) can be described as I in A♭ with the *root* as the lowest note, (b) as I with the *third* as the lowest note.

(a) (b) (c)

Using this method, describe chord (c) *I with the fifth as the lowest note.*

C A third way is to write first the letter name of the triad. After it a slash (/) is written, followed by the letter name of the pitch of the lowest note. In the chords in **B** above, (a) is A♭/A♭, (b) is A♭/C, (c) is A♭/E♭. In practice, root position chords as in (a) often have only the chord letter name, the slash and lowest note being omitted. Minor chords must have 'm' written after their letter name.

8 When describing triads, you may choose any of the methods above in your answer. But be prepared to meet any of the other methods used.

9 If you are asked to name a triad like the one on the right, work as follows:

Stage 1 See if it is a $\frac{5}{3}$, $\frac{6}{3}$ or $\frac{6}{4}$ chord. If it is not already a $\frac{5}{3}$ chord, rewrite its notes as one:

Stage 2 Look at the key signature and/or accidentals. Decide in which pair of major or relative minor keys the triad may be – here the keys are E♭ major or C minor.

Stage 3 Write out and label Ia, IIa, IVa and Va in both keys:

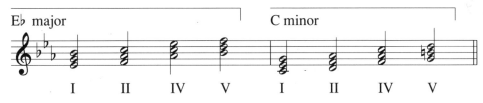

E♭ major

    I   II   IV   V

C minor

    I   II   IV   V

Stage 4 Write down the key, and the number of the chord, which is the same as the chord you have written in Stage 1. It is I in C minor.

Stage 5 Decide whether the chord given at the beginning of **9** is a $\frac{5}{3}$, $\frac{6}{3}$ or $\frac{6}{4}$ chord. It is a $\frac{6}{4}$ chord, so it is Ic in C minor.

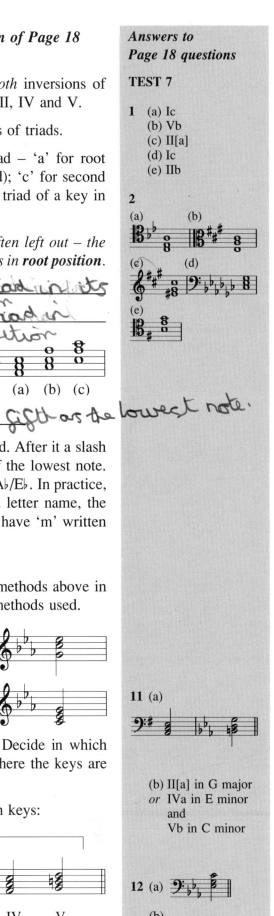

TEST 7

1 (a) Ic
   (b) Vb
   (c) II[a]
   (d) Ic
   (e) IIb

2
(a)   (b)

(c)   (d)

(e)

11 (a)

(b) II[a] in G major
or IVa in E minor
    and
    Vb in C minor

12 (a)

(b)

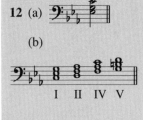

I II IV V

(c) Ib

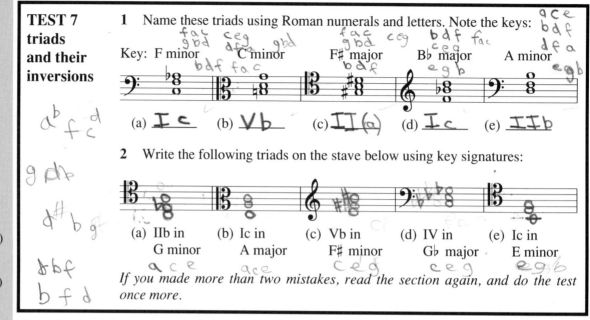

TEST 7 triads and their inversions

1 Name these triads using Roman numerals and letters. Note the keys:

Key: F minor   C minor   F# major   Bb major   A minor

(a) Ic   (b) Vb   (c) II(a)   (d) Ic   (e) IIb

2 Write the following triads on the stave below using key signatures:

(a) IIb in G minor
(b) Ic in A major
(c) Vb in F# minor
(d) IV in Gb major
(e) Ic in E minor

If you made more than two mistakes, read the section again, and do the test once more.

7 (a) Subdominant triad in 1st inversion ($^6_3$)

(b) Supertonic triad in root position ($^5_3$)

(c) I with the fifth as the lowest note

close and open position

10 All triads so far have been in **close position**, which means that all notes of the triads lie within an octave.

Triads where the range of notes is greater than an octave are said to be in **open position**. They may be written on more than one stave.

Here is Ia of C major, in close and then in two open positions.

All are in root position, because the bottom note in each is C.

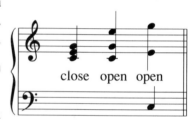

close open open

naming open triads

11 Before naming a chord in open position, rewrite the bass note at the same pitch. Then move the other notes down by octaves until the chord is in close position.

(a) Rewrite each of these triads in close position on the bass stave:

Follow the method in paragraph **9** to decide numbers and inversions.

(b) Identify each of these chords: ____II(a) in____ and ____Vb in C m____

G major

chords of four notes

12 A note of a triad may be written a second time (usually in a different octave) to make a *four* note chord. In this chord in C minor, C appears twice. To find out what triad it is formed from,

(a) write the notes as a close position triad in the bass clef after the chord.

Now use the method you were shown in 9 –

(b) Write out as $^5_3$ triads, I, II IV and V in C minor:

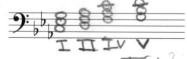

I   II   IV   V

(c) What is the number and inversion of the four-note chord? ____Ib?____

18

Look at the passage below in D major:

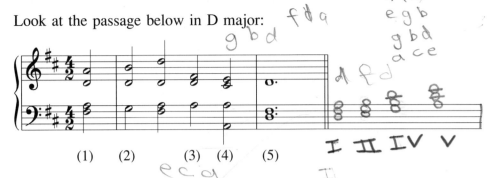

(1)   (2)   (3) (4)   (5)

(d) Write and label triads I, II, IV and V on the empty part of the stave.

(e) What are the numbers and letters for chords 1–5? _Ib, IV, Ic, V, I_

TEST 8
chords

For each of the three passages below:
(1) name the key of the music,
(2) write triads I, II, IV and V of that key on the empty part of the stave, and label these triads with their Roman numerals,
(3) identify each of the chords marked by bracketed letters.

1
Croft
Key: G major

(a) (b) (c)   (d)   (e)
I(a) IIb V(a)   Vb   IIb

2
Key: F minor

(a) IIb (b) Ic (c) V(a) (d) I(a)

3
Handel (adapted)
Key: A major

(a) (b)   (c) (d) (e)   (f)
I(a) Vb   IV II V Ib

If you made more than two mistakes, read 11 and 12 again and do the test once more.

13 Key: G major
(a) II
(b) IIb
(c) V
(d) I
(e) IV
(f) I

15 perfect

16 plagal

18 (a) D major
perfect

(b) C major
plagal

(c) G major
imperfect

19 (a) I[a]
(b) Ib
(c) Vb

20 (a) Ic
(b) perfect

**Answers to
Page 19 questions**

12 (d)

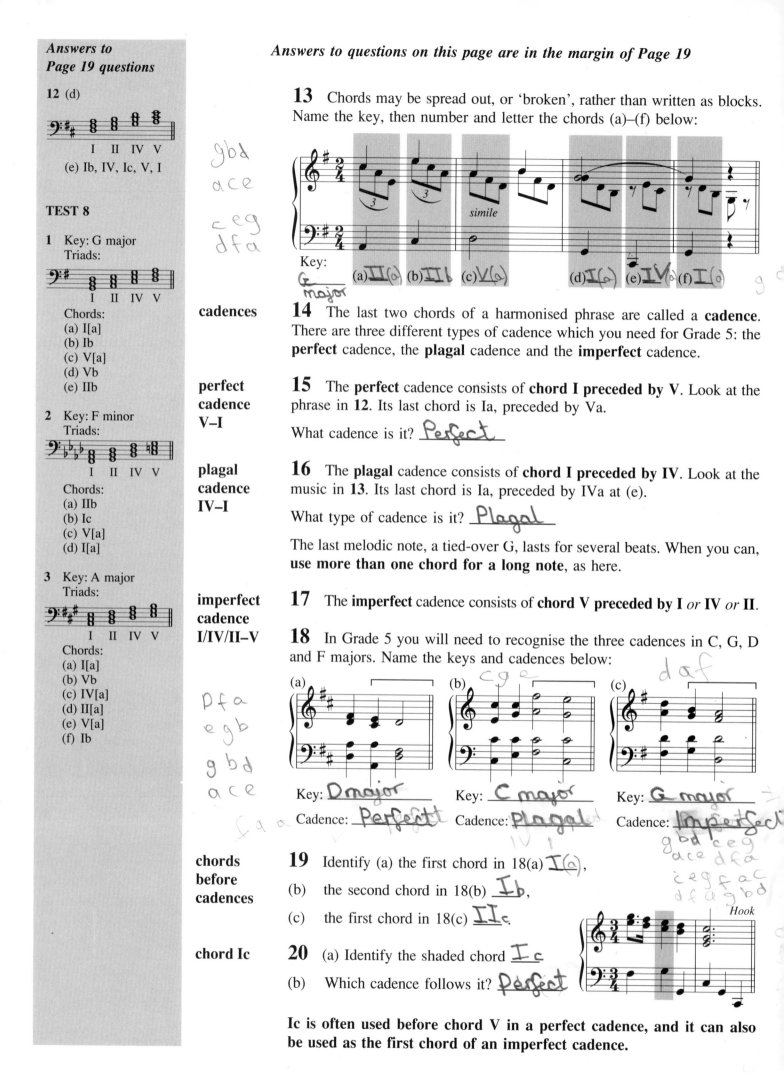

I   II   IV   V

(e) Ib, IV, Ic, V, I

TEST 8

1 Key: G major
Triads:

I   II   IV   V
Chords:
(a) I[a]
(b) Ib
(c) V[a]
(d) Vb
(e) IIb

2 Key: F minor
Triads:

I   II   IV   V
Chords:
(a) IIb
(b) Ic
(c) V[a]
(d) I[a]

3 Key: A major
Triads:

I   II   IV   V
Chords:
(a) I[a]
(b) Vb
(c) IV[a]
(d) II[a]
(e) V[a]
(f) Ib

13 Chords may be spread out, or 'broken', rather than written as blocks. Name the key, then number and letter the chords (a)–(f) below:

Key:
G major   (a) II (a)   (b) IIb   (c) V (a)   (d) I (a)   (e) IV (a)   (f) I (a)

cadences

14 The last two chords of a harmonised phrase are called a **cadence**. There are three different types of cadence which you need for Grade 5: the **perfect** cadence, the **plagal** cadence and the **imperfect** cadence.

**perfect
cadence
V–I**

15 The **perfect** cadence consists of **chord I preceded by V**. Look at the phrase in **12**. Its last chord is Ia, preceded by Va.

What cadence is it? Perfect

**plagal
cadence
IV–I**

16 The **plagal** cadence consists of **chord I preceded by IV**. Look at the music in **13**. Its last chord is Ia, preceded by IVa at (e).

What type of cadence is it? Plagal

The last melodic note, a tied-over G, lasts for several beats. When you can, **use more than one chord for a long note**, as here.

**imperfect
cadence
I/IV/II–V**

17 The **imperfect** cadence consists of **chord V preceded by I** *or* **IV** *or* **II**.

18 In Grade 5 you will need to recognise the three cadences in C, G, D and F majors. Name the keys and cadences below:

(a)   (b)   (c)

Key: D major   Key: C major   Key: G major
Cadence: Perfect   Cadence: Plagal   Cadence: Imperfect

**chords
before
cadences**

19 Identify (a) the first chord in 18(a) I (a),

(b)   the second chord in 18(b) Ib,

(c)   the first chord in 18(c) IIc.

chord Ic

20 (a) Identify the shaded chord Ic

(b)   Which cadence follows it? Perfect

Hook

Ic is often used before chord V in a perfect cadence, and it can also be used as the first chord of an imperfect cadence.

21 To find suitable chords for cadences, work in this way:

II IV I   II V I

(a) Find the key. What is it here? *C major*

(b) Write out triads I, II, IV and V in the bass clef. Number them.

I II IV V

Look at the cadence in bars 7–8.

(c) Which chords contain the note D (melody of bar 7)? *II + V*

(d) Which chords contain the note C (melody of bar 8)? *I + IV*
No cadence ends with chord IV, so you will need a perfect cadence.

(e) Which chord number must be written in bar 8? *I*

Look at the two melody notes D (bar 7). The second *must* be harmonised with chord V, because the cadence is perfect (V–I). The first melody note of this bar can be harmonised with *either* chord II *or* chord V.

(f) Write the chord numbers on the lines in bars 7–8.

Now look at the cadence in bars 3–4.

(g) Which chords contain the note G (melody of bar 4)? *I + V*

(h) Which chords contain the note A (melody of bar 3)? *II + IV*

The melody note of bar 4 is a note which is found in chord I.

There is a note from chord IV immediately preceding it, in bar 3.

(i) Which cadence uses both these chords? *Plagal*

(j) The G in bar 4 is *also* found in chord V. The A which precedes it is found in chords II and IV.

Which cadence ends with chord V? *Imperfect*

You may therefore choose *either* a plagal cadence in bars 3–4, *or* an imperfect cadence.

(k) Write the numbers of the chords you choose on the lines in bars 3–4.

22 Write in the brackets suitable cadence chords:

(a) IV I

(b) IV I

23 What chord would harmonise the first two notes of:

(c)

IV

(a)? *I*   (b)? *V or I*

(margin notes)
f a c
g b d

b d f →
c e g

d f a
e g b
g b d
a c e

c e g
d f a
f a c
g b d

I

Answers to
Page 21 questions

21 (a) C major

(b)

   I   II   IV   V

(c) II and V

(d) I and IV

(e) I

(f) II *or* V, V, I

(g) I and V

(h) II and IV

(i) plagal

(j) imperfect

(k) IV–I *or*
   II–V *or*
   IV–V

22 (a) IV–I *or*
   IV–V *or*
   II–V

(b) V–I

(c) I–V

23 (a) I

(b) I *or* V

In Grade 5, you must either compose a melody for given words, or continue an instrumental melody (for up to a total of eight bars).

The composition of melodies is one of the most interesting of all musical activities. **You must be able to hear accurately in your mind what you are writing. This skill comes only with practice. Write very simple melodies at first.**

composing songs

1 Here is a way of writing a very simple melody for the words

> *Tyger, Tyger burning bright*
> *In the forests of the night.*

Stage 1 Write a suitable rhythm. Several possibilities were discussed in *Theory Time!* Grade 4, pages 22 and 23. Read these pages again. One rhythm was:

Tyg- er, tyg - er burn- ing bright In __ the for- ests of __ the night.

Stage 2 Write the words under the staves first, to get correct spacing, dividing up separate syllables with hyphens. Number the bars.

Stage 3 The melody must reflect the general mood of the words being set. Read over the words very carefully. Decide a suitable tempo and if the key should be major or minor.

For this, a major key and a moderately fast tempo is acceptable. G major is chosen as a convenient key, but it can be transposed to suit a particular type of voice later.

Stage 4 Give the first *strong* accent the tonic note (G), or another note of chord I, to establish the key at the outset.

Stage 5 End the first half of the melody on a note of the dominant chord, to suggest an imperfect cadence. Write V over bar 4.

Stage 6 Compose a simple stepwise melody for bars 1–4, using the chosen rhythm. It starts on a note of chord I, and ends on a note of chord V.

Ty- ger, ty - ger burn- ing bright

Stage 7 The second half can also be stepwise. The *note before the last* should either be part of chord V to suggest a *perfect* cadence, or part of chord IV to suggest a *plagal* cadence.

The last note should be a note of chord I, and *not less than one beat long*. V and I are pencilled in over the last two notes.

Ty- ger, ty - ger burn- ing bright In _ the for- ests of _ the night.

Stage 8 Slur any groups of notes that are intended to be sung to the same syllable. If these slurs are over single-syllable words, the word will need a 'continuation line' (like the ones after *In* and *of* in bars 5 and 7). Put in a suitable tempo marking, and directions for dynamics, etc.

Stage 9 Check that the range is suitable for the type of voice you intend to perform the song. If it is not, transpose the melody.

2 Comfortable ranges for voices are shown below:

soprano   alto   tenor   bass

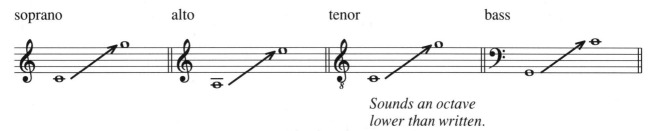

Sounds an octave
lower than written.

3 If you compose in a minor key you should use the melodic form. Remember that when this descends, the sixth and seventh degrees are as indicated by its key signature, but that when it ascends they are sharpened.

4 Once you are confident that you can hear what you write, compose more ambitious melodies. Experiment with leaps instead of stepwise movement, staring with intervals of a third, and try using plagal as well as perfect and imperfect cadences.

5 **Songs starting with an anacrusis.** The first strongly accented syllable should be set to a note of chord I of the chosen key. The weak syllable(s) before the first barline can be set to a note of chord V. A leap of dominant to tonic is very effective:

Allegro moderato

"Will you walk a lit - tle fas - ter," said the Whit - ing to the Snail,

6 Write melodies for the other words in Theory Time! Grade 4, pages 22 and 23. Here are two more verses to set as songs:

"Pipe a song about a Lamb!"	*The Owl and the Pussycat went to sea*
So I piped with merry cheer.	*In a beautiful pea-green boat.*
"Piper pipe that song again."	*They took some honey and plenty of money*
So I piped: he wept to hear.	*Wrapped up in a five-pound note.*
William Blake	Edward Lear

continuing instrumental melodies

1 When you are continuing an instrumental melody of which the beginning is given, you have more freedom than in songs, where the rhythms are determined by the words.

However, you must be influenced in your rhythm by the given start. See pages 27 and 28 of *Theory Time!* Grade 3.

2 The key in which you must work is determined by the opening you are given. You must know the range of the instrument for which you are composing.

The table below shows the lowest useful note of the commonest instruments. These notes are at concert pitch. All the instruments can play notes comfortably for a minimum of two octaves above their lowest note – stay within this range at first, unless there is a note to the contrary on the table.

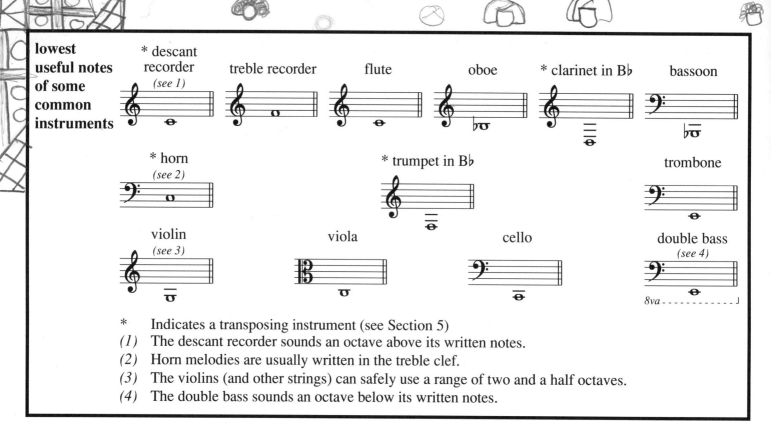

	*descant recorder	treble recorder	flute	oboe	*clarinet in B♭	bassoon
lowest useful notes of some common instruments	(see 1)					

* horn (see 2)   * trumpet in B♭   trombone

violin (see 3)   viola   cello   double bass (see 4)

*   Indicates a transposing instrument (see Section 5)
(1)   The descant recorder sounds an octave above its written notes.
(2)   Horn melodies are usually written in the treble clef.
(3)   The violins (and other strings) can safely use a range of two and a half octaves.
(4)   The double bass sounds an octave below its written notes.

3   The general style of the given opening, as well as its rhythm, should be continued in the melody.

4   Suppose it is necessary to continue this opening for violin to make a melody of eight bars:

Stage 1   Prepare a stave with the given opening. Insert barlines and number bars.

Stage 2   Write V over the end of the first half (bar 4), I over the last bar, and V over the end of bar 7.

Stage 3   Continue the melody in the style of the opening until the end of bar 4. The last note should be a note of V, and lengthened to indicate a mid-way resting point:

Stage 4   In the second half of the melody, the rhythm of the opening is used again, but varied a little in bars 6 and 7. Stepwise movement is used. The last two notes are from the dominant and tonic chords of the key respectively.

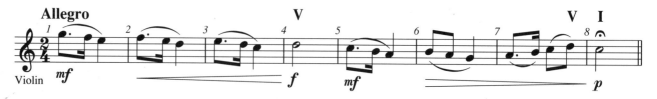

Stage 5   Insert performance directions suitable for the instrument for which you are writing.

5   Here are some more beginnings of melodies for you to continue:

24

Answers to questions on this page are in the margin of Page 26

Answers to
Page 26 questions

1 In Grade 4, you had to be able to recognise signs for ornaments. Revise carefully pages 25–27 in *Theory Time!* Grade 4.

TEST 9 revision of ornament signs

For which ornaments are the following the signs? (Specify position of turns – e.g. *Turn after note*, etc.)

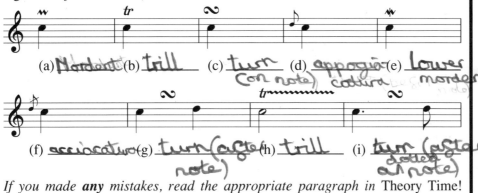

(a) ~~Mordent~~ (b) trill (c) turn (on note) (d) ~~appogia~~ cattura (e) Lower mordent

(f) ~~acciacatura~~ (g) turn (after note) (h) trill (i) turn (after dotted note)

*If you made **any** mistakes, read the appropriate paragraph in* Theory Time! *Grade 4 again.*

2 In Grade 5, you must be able to recognise written-out ornaments in a piece of music. The ornamentation of a note is a complicated matter. Much depends on the particular situation of the ornamented note in the music, the period in which the music was written, and a number of other matters. The information below should be sufficient for Grade 5.

3 Look at this table, which shows some ways in which ornaments can be written out.

acciaccatura

An acciaccatura can be played: (1) on the beat *with* the principal note and immediately released; (2) it can take its time from the principal note, which is shortened; (3) it can take its time from the *previous* note.

appoggiatura

The appoggiatura is played on the beat of the principal note. It always takes at least half the value of the principal note, and may take more.

upper and lower mordent

upper mordent   *lower mordent*

Mordents have three notes. Both upper and lower start and end on the principal note. The middle note of an upper mordent is the note *above* the principal note. The middle note of a lower mordent is the note *below* the principal note.

TEST 10

(a)
(b)
(c)
(d)
(e)

turns	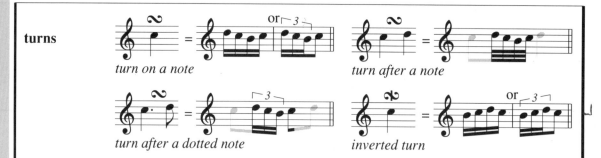

Turns have four notes: the note *above* the principal note, the principal note, the note *below* the principal note, then the principal note again. In an **inverted turn**, the first note is the note *below* the principal note, and the third note is the note *above* the principal note.

trills	

Trills consist of an alternation of the principal note and the note above it, with the last but one note usually the note *below* the principal note. A trill may end with a turn shape.

accidentals	Signs for mordents, turns and trill may have an accidental above them. This accidental affects the note *above* the principal note – for example, ♯ means that the note must be sharpened. Similarly, an accidental *below* the sign, for example ♯, changes the note *below* the principal note.

6 Notice that a note with an acciaccatura or an appoggiatura before it becomes, when written out fully, a group of *two* notes; a note with a mordent over it becomes a group of *three* notes; a note with a turn becomes a group of *four* notes. A written-out group of *five* notes may be a turn after a note or trill; *six* notes or more is likely to be a trill.

**TEST 10
ornaments**

Write out on the blank staves each of the groups of notes in a shaded box as a single note (the principal note) with appropriate ornament sign.

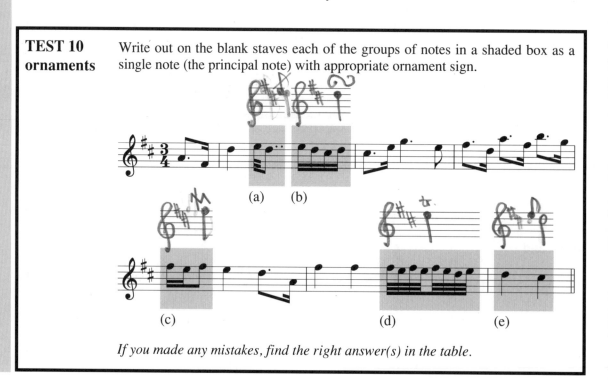

If you made any mistakes, find the right answer(s) in the table.

A Vocal Scores

1 Music for choirs is written in a number of vocal parts. The most usual number is four – soprano, alto, tenor and bass.

In a **vocal score**, the music for each part is written on a separate stave. Sopranos and altos sing from music in the treble clef. The tenor part also has music in the treble clef, but it is sung an octave lower than the written pitch – the treble clef at the start of a tenor stave often has a small *8* printed below it. Basses sing from music in the bass clef. Below is part of a vocal score of music by Handel:

Answers to
Page 28 questions

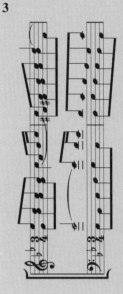

2 A vocal score can be rewritten as a **short score**, in which there are only two staves. Music for sopranos and altos is written on the upper stave, which uses the treble clef. Music for tenors and basses is written on the lower stave, using the bass clef. Here is the vocal score from **1**, rewritten as a short score:

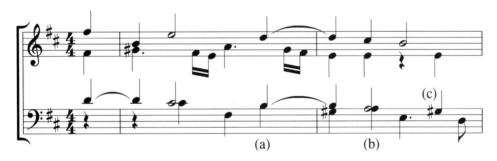

1 Notes of the soprano part are written on the upper stave *with all stems ascending*. Slurs and ties curve upwards.

2 Notes of the alto part are written on the upper stave *with all stems descending*. Slurs and ties curve downwards.

3 Notes of the tenor part are written on the lower stave, **at concert pitch in the bass clef**, *with all stems ascending*. Slurs and ties curve upwards.

4 Notes of the bass part are written on the lower stave *with all stems descending*. Slurs and ties curve downwards.

5 Two notes of identical pitch and value, but sounded by different parts at the same time, are written as at (a). If the two notes have different value (or are a step apart in pitch), they are staggered, as at (b).

6 Accidentals must appear in each voice part even if, at at (c), the same accidental has previously been inserted in the same bar for another voice.

7 Rests will sometimes need to be moved up or down from their normal position, as in the alto part of the last bar, to allow room for the other part on the stave. If both the parts on the stave have rests at the same time, two rest signs will be needed, positioned one above the other.

3 Rewrite these bars in short score:

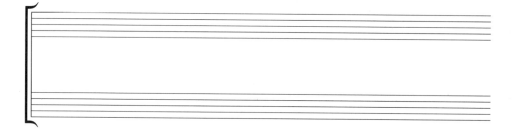

B Instrumental Scores

In Grade 5 questions you may see scores for various instrumental ensembles, though you will not be required to rewrite them into short score form. The most usual are scores for duos (e.g. cello and piano), trios and quartets.

They are similar to the vocal score shown above. Each instrument is given a separate stave in the same way that the different voices have separate staves, except that keyboard instruments require *two* staves – one for the right hand and one for the left.

The name of the instrument which is to play each stave is shown at the start, though you may be expected to know that the four instruments of a standard string quartet are first violin, second violin, viola and cello.

Section 10 – Terms & Signs

Answers to questions on this page are in the margin of page 30

Italian, French and German terms

1 A list of Italian, French and German terms and their meanings is printed on pages 32 and 33. Terms which are new for Grade 5 are underlined. Learn the new terms set, and revise those you learned for Grades 1–4.

2 To help you become familiar with the new German terms, complete the columns in this table.

Column A: German	Column B: Italian	Column C: English
(a) *mässig*	_____	_____
(b) _____	*largo*	_____
(c) _____	_____	without
(d) _____	*poco*	_____
(e) *lebhaft*	_____	_____
(f) _____	*dolente*	_____
(g) _____	_____	always
(h) _____	*dolce*	_____
(i) *mit Ausdruck*	_____	_____
(j) _____	*tranquillo*	_____
(k) _____	_____	tender
(l) *fröhlich*	_____	_____

new signs

3 There are a number of new signs you should know for Grade 5.

rests longer than a bar

Rests of more than one bar's length are shown by either of the methods below, the number of bars involved being written above.

3 bars' rest   *or*   3 bars' rest   7 bars' rest   *or*   7 bars' rest

repeated notes

4 Signs for groups of identical notes can be used. Sign (a) shows that quavers are to be played to fill the time taken by a crotchet; sign (b) that semiquavers are to be played to fill the time taken by a minim. The **head** shows the *total* length; the **beams** are those of the notes played. Repeated pairs of notes are shown in a similar way (c):

(a) *played as:* (b) *played as:* (c) *played as:*

5 Repeated chords can be indicated as shown at (d), with a stroke for each reiteration. (e) is the sign for a complete repeated bar and (f) is the sign to repeat the *two* previous bars. For repeated sections, see page 34.

(d) *played as:* (e) (f)

1 (a) violin

(b) violin

(c) viola

(d) cello

2 $\frac{2}{2}$ (*or* $\frac{4}{4}$)

3 (a) B♭ minor

(b) major 9th *or* compound major 2nd

(c) minor 2nd

4 (a) pluck the notes

(b) play the notes with the bow

(c) slow down a little

(d) return to the previous speed

5 (a) G♭

(b) E♭

(c) D♭, C, G♭

6 The note above the principal note in the trill is to be C♭

7 (a) perfect

(b) imperfect

8

29

Answers to questions on this page are in the margin of Page 29

Answers to Page 29 questions

2 (a) *mässig*
       moderato
       moderate

   (b) *langsam*
       largo
       slow

   (c) *ohne*
       senza
       without

   (d) *wenig*
       poco
       little

   (e) *lebhaft*
       vivace
       lively

   (f) *traurig*
       dolente
       sad

   (g) *immer*
       sempre
       always

   (h) *süss*
       dolce
       sweet

   (i) *mit Ausdruck*
       con espressione
       or *espressivo*
       with expression

   (j) *ruhig*
       tranquillo
       peaceful, tranquil

   (k) *zart*
       affetuoso
       tender

   (l) *fröhlich*
       giocoso
       joyful

Now that you have come to the end of this book, you will be able to understand more about the pieces of music you play, sing, or compose yourself. See if you can answer these questions about the piece of music on page 31. It is the end of a movement by Beethoven, written for string quartet.

1 What instrument plays the music on

   (a) the top stave? _____

   (b) the second stave down? _____

   (c) the third stave down? _____

   (d) the bottom stave? _____

2 The tempo marking for this piece is *presto*.
   What time signature would be most appropriate? ____

3 (a) Identify the key in bar 17 _____

   (b) Name the interval between the notes in the bracket marked *(x)* _____

   (c) Name the interval between the notes in the bracket marked *(y)* _____

4 What are the meanings of

   (a) *pizz.* in bar 9? _____

   (b) *arco* in bar 15? _____

   (c) *poco rit.* in bar 15? _____

   (d) *a tempo* in bar 17? _____

5 (a) What is the letter name of the highest note in the music? ____

   (b) What is the letter name of the lowest note in the music? ____

   (c) What are the letter names of the notes in the third stave down of bar 1?

       ____ ____ ____

6 What is the meaning of the flat sign written above the trill sign in bar 5?

   _____

7 Name the cadence in (a) bar 8 _____

   (b) bar 11 (last crotchet, which is chord II, second inversion) to bar 12 _____

8 Write out bars 9–12 of the top stave for clarinet in B♭. The interval of transposition is a major second higher. Remember to write the new key signature.

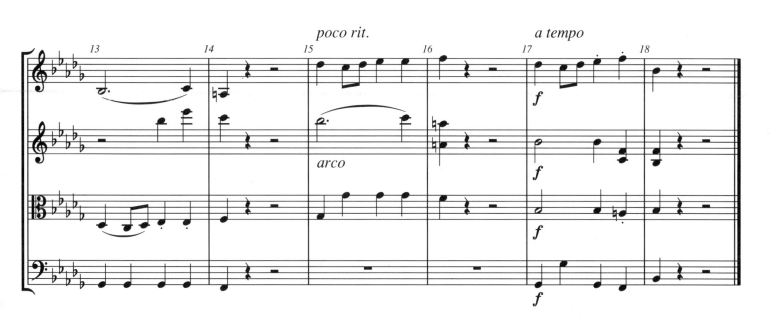

Table of Musical Terms & Signs

1 Italian Terms — New terms for Grade 5 are <u>underlined</u>

Tempo

a tempo	in time (*tempo* means time)
adagietto	slow, but less slow than *adagio*
adagio	slow, leisurely
allegro	fairly fast
allegretto	fairly fast, but less fast than *allegro*
andante	at a moderate walking pace
andantino	a little faster than *andante*
grave	very slow and solemn
larghetto	fairly slow
largo	slow and dignified, broad
lento	slow
misura, alla	strict time
misura, senza	without time (i.e. in free time)
moderato	at a moderate speed
presto	fast
tempo comodo	at a comfortable speed
veloce	swiftly
vivace, vivo	fast and lively

Changes to Tempo

accelerando	getting faster gradually
affretando	hurrying
allargando	broadening – slower
doppio movimento	twice as quickly
incalzando	getting quicker
rallentando (rall.)	getting slower gradually
ritardando (ritard.)	getting slower gradually
ritenuto (rit.)	holding back
rubato, tempo rubato	with some freedom in time
stringendo	gradually getting faster
tenuto (ten.)	held

Dynamics

forte (**f**)	loud
forte piano (**fp**)	loud, then immediately soft
fortissimo (**ff**)	very loud
mezzo forte (**mf**)	moderately loud
piano (**p**)	quiet
pianissimo (**pp**)	very quiet
mezzo piano (**mp**)	moderately quiet

Changes to Dynamics

calando, morendo	dying away gradually
perdendosi	dying away gradually
crescendo (cresc.)	gradually getting louder
decrescendo	gradually getting quieter
diminuendo (dim.)	gradually getting quieter
rinforzando (**rf. rfz.**)	stressed or accented
smorzando	dying away to nothing
sforzato, sforzando	accented loudly (**sf** or **sfz**)

Manner of Performance

ad libitum	freely, as you wish
affetuoso	tenderly, gently
agitato	agitated
amabile	loving
amore, con amore	with love
animato	animated and lively
appassionato	with passion
arco	bow the notes
attacca	go straight on
brio, con	with vigour
cantabile, cantando	in a singing style
deciso, con deciso	with decision
delicato, con delicato	with delicacy
dolce	sweetly
dolente, doloroso	sadly
dolore, con	with sadness
energico, con	with energy
espressivo	expressively
forza, con forza	with force
fuoco, con fuoco	with fire
giocoso	playful
grazioso	graceful
lacrimoso	sad, tearful
largamente	broadly
legato	smoothly
leggiero	lightly
lusingando	in a persuasive way
maestoso	majestic
marcato	marked
marziale	in a martial style
mesto	sad
moto, mosso	movement
nobilmente	broad and noble
pesante	heavy
piacevole	pleasantly
piangevole	plaintively
pizzicato (pizz.)	pluck the notes
risoluto, con	with determination
ritmico	rhythmically
scherzando, scherzoso	playful, joking
segue	continue
semplice	simple, uncomplicated
sonoro	resonant
sordini, con sordini	with mutes
sostenuto	sustained
staccato	sharp, detached
teneramente	tenderly
tranquillo	tranquil, calm
triste, tristamente	sad, sorrowful
volante	fast and flying

Other

da capo (D.C.)	(repeat) from the beginning
dal segno (D.S.)	(repeat) from the sign
fine	end
prima volta	first time
seconda volta	second time

32

Qualifying words

al, alla	in the manner of		*pochettino*	a very little
assai	very		*poco*	a little or slightly (*poco crescendo* – getting slightly louder)
come	like			
con	with		*possibile*	possible
e, ed	and		*quasi*	like, in the manner of
facile	easy		*sempre*	always
giusto	exact		*senza*	without
lunga	long (*lunga pausa* – long pause)		*simile*	in the same way
ma	but		*sopra*	above
meno	less		*sotto*	below
molto	very or much (*molto piano* – very quiet)		*stesso*	the same (*l'istesso* or *lo stesso*)
niente	nothing		*subito*	suddenly
non	not		*troppo*	too much
ossia	or		*tanto*	so much
più	more		*voce*	voice (*sotto voce* – in an undertone)

2   French Terms

à	to, at		*moins*	less
animé	animated and lively		*non*	not
assez	fairly		*peu*	little
avec	with		*plus*	more
cédez	get slower		*presser*	hurry
douce	sweetly		*ralentir*	to slow down
en dehors	prominent		*retenu*	held back
et	and		*sans*	without (*sans sourdines* – without mutes)
légèrement	lightly		*très*	very
lent	slow		*un, une*	one
mais	but		*vif, vive*	lively
modéré	at a moderate speed		*vite*	quick

3   German Terms

All new in Grade 5

aber	but		*ohne*	without (*Ohne Dämpfer* – without mutes)
Ausdruck	expression		*ruhig*	peaceful
bewegt	with movement, urgently		*schnell*	quickly
breit	broad		*sehr*	very
ein, eine	a, one		*retenu*	held back
einfach	simple		*süss*	sweet
etwas	rather		*traurig*	sad
fröhlich	joyful		*und*	and
immer	always		*voll*	full
langsam	slow		*wenig*	little
lebhaft	lively		*wieder*	again
mässig	at a moderate speed		*zart*	tender
mit	with		*zu*	to (= towards), too (= also)
nicht	not			

Signs used in Music

 is often used for *crescendo*.

is often used for *diminuendo*.

A dot over or under a note means that the note is to be played staccato:

If staccato notes are slurred, they should be played semi-staccato – not as short as ordinary staccato notes.

A triangle ▼ means a very sharp staccato.

A > sign over or under a note means that the note must be accented. The sign ∧ means an even stronger accent:

The sign ⌢ over or under a note means that the performer should pause on the note:

MM is short for Maelzel's Metronome. The performer is to set the metronome to the number which follows. If the direction is, for example, MM ♩ = 60, it means that there should be sixty crotchet beats to the minute.

8va- - - - - - - - - - - ⌐ over a group of notes means that you must play the marked note an octave higher. The sign *8va - - - - - - ⌐* written under notes means that the notes must be played an octave lower.

A slur over or under a group of notes means that the notes should be played *legato* – in other words, joined together. Don't confuse this sign with the tie, which links together two notes of the same pitch.

The marks at the end mean that you must go back to the first marks, and repeat the music between the marks.

1. or *prima volta* means that the marked bar is to be played when the passage is played for the first time.
2. or *seconda volta* means that the marked bar is to be played instead of the bar marked **1** when the passage is repeated.

The marking 𝄢ed. ✳ or 𝓛_____ shows where the right piano pedal is to be put down, and released.
Note that the first repeat sign ‖:, at the *beginning* of a piece may be omitted.

The signs ⊓ and ∨ in music for strings show the direction of the bow —
⊓ means bow from heel to tip (down bow); ∨ means bow from tip to heel (up bow).

Music engraving and typesetting by
Musonix, London

Printed by
Halstan & Co. Ltd., Amersham, Bucks. England

12/04 (53406)